ILLUSTRATED GAMES OF PATIENCE

ILLUSTRATED GAMES OF PATIENCE

BY LADY ADELAIDE CADOGAN

DEDICATED BY PERMISSION

TO

HIS ROYAL HIGHNESS PRINCE LEOPOLD, K.G.

"How poor are they that have not patience"—OTHELLO

Patientia vincit

PRENTICE-HALL, Inc., Englewood Cliffs, N.J.

© THIS EDITION LESLIE FREWIN PUBLISHERS LIMITED IN ASSOCIATION
WITH JOHN HUNTER AND ABACUS AG, 1968

Published in England by Leslie Frewin

First American Edition published by Prentice-Hall, Inc., 1969

13-451096-8

Library of Congress Catalog Card Number 75-80771

Printed in England
T

CONTENTS

PREFACE

LADY ADELAIDE CADOGAN, daughter of the 1st Marquess of Anglesey, and wife of the youngest son of the 3rd Earl of Cadogan, is the patron saint of Patience and the authoress of its 'bible', the *Illustrated Games of Patience*, published about 1870.

Her Ladyship seems to have been a fairly typical example of upper-class Victorian womanhood: something of a blue-stocking, lively, intelligent, and enough of a cosmopolitan to leave the charming titles of the games in their original French. The fact that her husband, William Frederick Cadogan, was a Member of Parliament suggests that we may owe the book partly to late-night sittings of the House of Commons.

By the 1870s, Patience was already a popular pastime, and it is surprising to learn that Lady Adelaide's compilation was the first on the subject to appear in the English language. Her name on the title page made the game fashionable overnight, and gave it the aristocratic stamp it still bears.

Illustrated Games of Patience became, and remained, a best seller. It has been reprinted many times, but without the elegant and colourful plates that made it *the* coffee-table book of London society during the latter half of Queen Victoria's reign and throughout that of Edward VII.

The rare copy, of which the present edition is a facsimile, was discovered only a year ago on just such a table in the home of a friend, Mrs Cicely Meredith. The book delighted me so much that I decided then and there to republish it, if it could be exactly reproduced. The generosity of Mrs Meredith and the skill of the printers have now made that possible.

I, therefore, gratefully dedicate this little exercise in nostalgia to them and to Dame Margaret Rutherford who so kindly and unexpectedly agreed to grace the book with her own characteristic observations on the game.

But first and last, of course, our thanks and homage must go to Lady Adelaide herself.

John Hunter

FOREWORD

BY DAME MARGARET RUTHERFORD, O.B.E.

They call it Patience—you play Patience and, often enough, when you play it you put yourself for all practical purposes into a condition or persuasion of patience. I suppose we have all, at some time or other, laid out the cards, in our Nursery, in sickness, or at one of those desperate moments of suspense before action, when all preparations have been made, every step been taken, and found we are committed and all that remains is to await the call.

One of my most vivid recollections, at the very outset of my career, passing down the corridor on my way to the stage was to see, through an open door, the great Marie Tempest at her table with the cards spread out. She was supreme, glittering and efficient, yet at repose, collected and ready to spring.

But one is not alone when one plays Patience. There is an invisible Opponent—yet a Comrade! This book presents a picture of him. From lonely Palaces in the Courts of Idleness? Who can say? From some hidden corner of Royal anxiety? From some bereft age when loved ones were a-far in Battle?

I feel a history in this book, and yet it is a picture of a formal, little, courteous Comfort, a quiet, inner Amusement.

Margaret Rutherford.

EXPLANATION OF THE TABLEAUX

THE blank spaces show where the foundation cards should be played during the deal.

When they are taken from the pack to form part of the original tableau the proper cards are painted.

EXPLANATION OF TERMS

Available cards. Those that are not "blocked" by other cards, *i.e.* not forbidden by the particular rules of each game, to be used.

Released cards. Those which, by the removal of the cards that blocked them, have now become available.

Suitable cards. Those whose value and suit fit them to be played or placed in the tableaux.

Foundation cards. Those on which the Patience is formed. These are generally aces and kings.

Marriage. The placing a card *of the same suit* on the next one above or below it in value. Any number may be placed on each other in this way.

Sequence. The regular succession of cards ascending from ace to king, or descending from king to ace; a sequence need not be of one suit.

Value. The figures of the court cards, and the number of points of the minor ones.

Suit. Either hearts, spades, diamonds, or clubs.

Lane. An empty space in the tableau, which has been formed by the removal of an entire row of cards.

Talon. Cards which, being unsuitable at the moment, are laid aside in one or more packets till they can come into use.

To play cards. The *placing them on the foundations* in contradistinction to placing them elsewhere.

Re-deal. These are always in addition to the original deal.

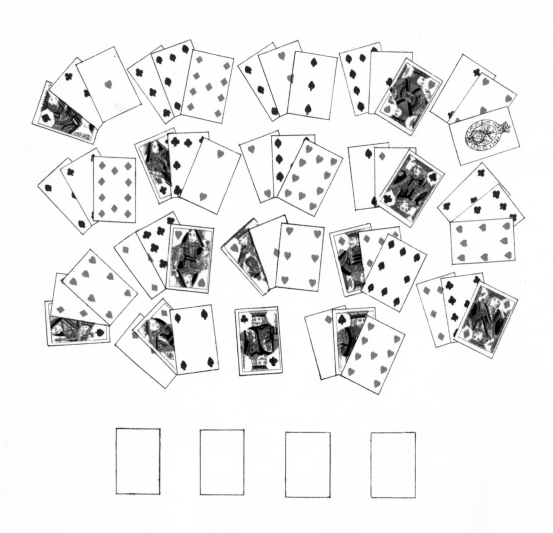

LA BELLE LUCIE

Vincent Brooks Day & Son Lith.

LA BELLE LUCIE.

One entire Pack of Cards.

RULES.

I. THE uppermost card of each packet is alone available, until by its removal it releases the one beneath.

II. The foundations must follow suit.

PLAY.

Deal out the entire pack in packets of three cards dealt together and placed as in tableau. The last packet, however, will contain but one card.

The four aces form the foundation cards, and are to ascend in sequence to kings.

Having placed the tableau, take any aces that may appear on the surface of the packets and play them in their allotted spaces, and upon them any other suitable cards, subject to Rule I.

When all available cards have been played, you proceed to release others, by forming marriages in a descending line on the tableau; but great care is requisite, lest in releasing one card another still more necessary to success should be blocked. The whole tableau should be carefully examined, and the combinations arranged so as to release the greatest number of suitable cards.

When this has been done, and that there are no more available cards to play, the entire tableau may be taken up, shuffled and re-dealt (if necessary twice), then played again as before.

This game can also be played with two packs, the eight aces forming the foundation cards, and double the number of packets being dealt for the tableau. It is then called " THE HOUSE IN THE WOOD."

There is also another way of playing it with two packs. The foundation cards to be four aces, and four kings of different suits, and marriages made both in ascending and descending lines. The name of this game is " THE HOUSE ON THE HILL."

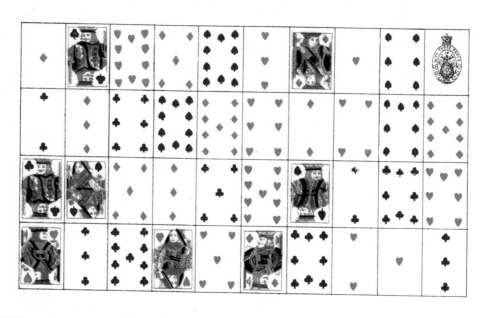

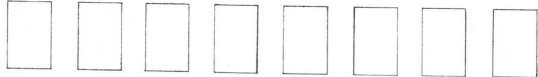

LE CADRAN.

Vincent Brooks Day & Son Lith

LE CADRAN.

Two Entire Packs of Cards.

RULES.

I.   ONLY cards in the lowest row are available, until a card in any other row is released by the removal of those below it, the principle being that *no card can be used that has another below it.*

II.   The foundations must follow suit.

PLAY.

Deal out from left to right four rows of ten cards.

The eight aces, when they can be placed, form the foundation cards, and are to ascend in sequence to kings.

Should any aces appear in the lowest row, play them in their allotted spaces, and upon them any suitable cards to continue the foundations (Rule I.)

You must now examine the tableau and endeavour by forming marriages (in descending line, and always subject to Rule I.) to release other suitable cards.   This, however, must be done with care, lest a sequence in a lower row may block a card above it which is much wanted, and might soon have been released.

If by these changes you can make a vacancy in the uppermost

row (thus forming a perpendicular lane), it is of the greatest use. The vacancy may be re-filled with any available card from the tableau or from the talon, but you are not obliged to re-fill it until a favourable opportunity occurs.

Note.—Some players only allow the vacancy to be filled from the talon.

The card so placed has all the privileges of the original card whose place it fills, and is treated in the same manner.

When there are no more available cards to play, proceed to deal out the remainder of the pack, turning the cards one by one, playing all suitable ones on the foundations, or placing them on the sequences of the tableau. The cards that cannot be so employed are laid aside in one packet forming the talon.

There is no re-deal.

L A   Q U I N Z A I N E .

LA QUINZAINE.

Two Entire Packs of Cards.

RULES.

I. ONLY cards in the seventh or lowest row are available, until by their removal those above them are released. *No card can at any time be used that has any other below it.*

Note.—There is one exception to this rule, in case the game cannot be opened. See below.

II. Each foundation must follow suit.

PLAY.

Deal out the entire pack from left to right, in horizontal rows, fifteen cards in each, excepting the last one, which can only contain fourteen. Each row should partly cover over the preceding one; four aces and four kings form the foundation cards, the aces ascending in sequence to kings, the kings descending in sequence to aces. *When the deal is complete*, if any foundation cards should appear in the lowest row (Rule I.) play them at once on the spaces reserved, and also any other suitable cards—then marry, both in ascending and in descending lines, subject to Rule I. ; but if, after these changes, no foundation card is available, so that the patience cannot even begin, you may withdraw from the sixth row one ace and one king, if any are to be found (see note to Rule I.) immediately filling the spaces so made with the cards below which had previously blocked them. If even this resource is unavailing, the patience has already failed, there being no re-deal, and no further infringement of rules allowed.

When one or more foundations are established, examine the tableau carefully, marry all available cards, and endeavour by these changes to release the greatest number of suitable cards for the foundations, and to open out one or more perpendicular lanes. These are of the greatest use ; you may select any available card and place it at the top of the lane, and below it any others in sequence of the same suit, each card partly concealing the preceding one, as in the original deal.

You may also use the lane for reversing any sequences previously made. Thus, supposing there is a sequence beginning with a ten and ending with a three (the ten being required for one of the foundations), place the three at the top of the lane, the other cards following until the ten becomes the lowest or available card.

In theory this patience is simple, but it is very difficult to play. The combinations are endless, from the constant reversing of sequences, and require great attention. As the success principally depends on the lanes, it is more prudent, when you have only one, not to re-fill it until by some fresh combination you can open out another one.

There is no re-deal.

LA LOI SALIQUE.

Vincent Brooks Day & Son Lith.

LA LOI SALIQUE.

Two Entire Packs of Cards.

RULES.

I. Only the cards on the surface of the king packets are available, until their removal as usual releases those beneath, but all the cards in each packet may be examined.

II. The foundations do not follow suit.

PLAY.

Take from the pack and place one king to begin the line of eight kings, that are to be successively placed in a horizontal row as they appear in the deal. On this first king you place all the cards as you deal them until the next king appears. You now place the cards as you deal them upon this second king, and you continue thus to deal out the whole pack, always heaping upon the last king that has appeared all the cards as they are dealt.

The eight aces are to form the foundation cards, and are to ascend in sequence to knaves (Rule II.) When in the course of the deal any aces appear, they are to be immediately placed in a line above the king packets, and upon them any suitable cards (Rule I.), and when the queens appear they are to be placed in a row above the foundations. The queens are merely placed to complete the final tableau, which if the patience succeeds, consists of the eight queens above, the eight knaves finishing the foundations in the centre, and the eight kings below. You must continually examine the surface of the king packets to play any suitable cards on the foundations, and in so doing endeavour to free some of the kings entirely, for when the deal is ended you are allowed to place one card from any of the other packets (Rule I.) on each king, and you must of course choose those cards that will release the greatest number of suitable cards for the foundations, for which purpose the whole packets may be examined.   In this consists the entire play.

There is no re-deal.

LES QUATRE COINS.

LES QUATRE COINS.

Two Entire Packs of Cards.

RULES.

I. AFTER the deal is completed, the uppermost card of each packet is available and may be placed on *any of the foundations*, the cards underneath being released as usual by the removal of those that covered them.

II. Each foundation must follow suit.

PLAY.

Deal out twelve cards as in tableau, beginning on the left. Place the top corner card, then the four side cards, lastly the lower corner card; repeat this process on the right hand, beginning with the top corner, and leaving space in the centre for the foundation cards. These will consist of four aces and four kings of different suits, the aces ascending in sequence to kings, and the kings descending in sequence to aces.

Having dealt the first round of twelve cards, proceed to deal out the entire pack in successive rounds covering the first one, but in dealing each several round the following method must be strictly observed.

The eight foundation cards as they appear in the deal (whether they fall on the corner or on the side packets) are to be at once played in the space reserved for them, and on these may be played any suitable cards which in dealing fall *on either of the four corner packets;* but when a card (otherwise suitable) falls on either of the *side packets* it may not be played unless the foundation to which it belongs happens to be the one *immediately adjoining the side packet on which that card fell in dealing.*

Note.—Whenever in dealing a card is withdrawn, to place on one of the foundations, the next card in the pack is placed in its stead.

After the entire deal is completed these restrictions cease, all suitable cards may now be played, subject to Rule I., and marriages, both in ascending and descending lines, may be made with cards on the surface of the twelve packets; great care must, however, be taken in making these marriages, lest in releasing one card you block another that is equally required. The contents of each packet should be carefully examined, and only those marriages made which release the greatest number of suitable cards.

Note.—The sequences thus made may be reversed if required, viz. if one of the packets contained a sequence, beginning with deuce and ascending to eight (this being of course the top card) and one of the other packets had at the top a nine of the same suit, the eight might be placed on the nine, the rest of the sequence following, till the deuce became the top (or available card).

When all possible combinations have been made, and further progress is impossible, the twelve packets may be taken up in order, beginning on the left, re-dealt, and played exactly as before. If necessary, there may be two re-deals.

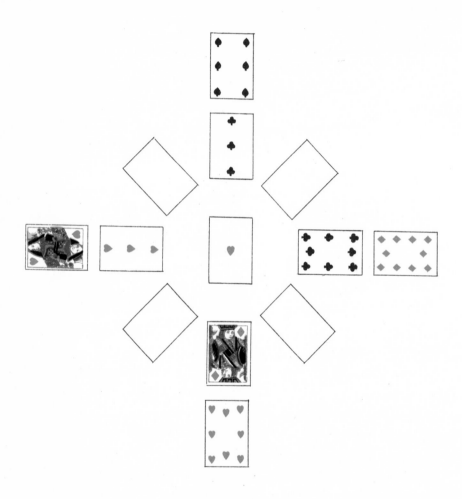

LE MOULIN.

LE MOULIN.

Two Entire Packs of Cards.

RULES.

I.   ALL cards in the wings are available.

II.   The five foundations do not follow suit.

PLAY.

Take from the pack one ace and place it in the centre before you; next deal out eight cards, grouping them round the ace to represent the wings of a windmill. The *first four kings* that appear in dealing are to be played in the four angles (see tableau). These, with the centre ace, form the five foundation cards. Each of the four kings is to descend in sequence to ace, while upon the centre ace four entire families are to be piled in sequences (Rule II.).

Having placed the centre ace and the wings, take from the latter any kings for the foundations, or other suitable cards to play on them, or on the centre ace, filling up the spaces so made from the cards in your hand. Then proceed to deal out the remaining cards, turning them one by one, playing all whose value admit of it on the foundations. The cards that cannot be so used are placed aside in one packet forming the talon.

Note.—The four families on the centre ace each begin with ace and end with king.

It is better to play cards from the talon rather than from the wings.

Vacancies in the wings must be *immediately* re-filled from the pack or talon.

In forming the foundations, the uppermost card of either of the king packets may be transferred, if suitable, to the ace packet; but this privilege is limited to *one* card of each at a time, and may only be resorted to when the playing of that card would bring into immediate use any other available card of the wings or of the talon.

There is no re-deal.

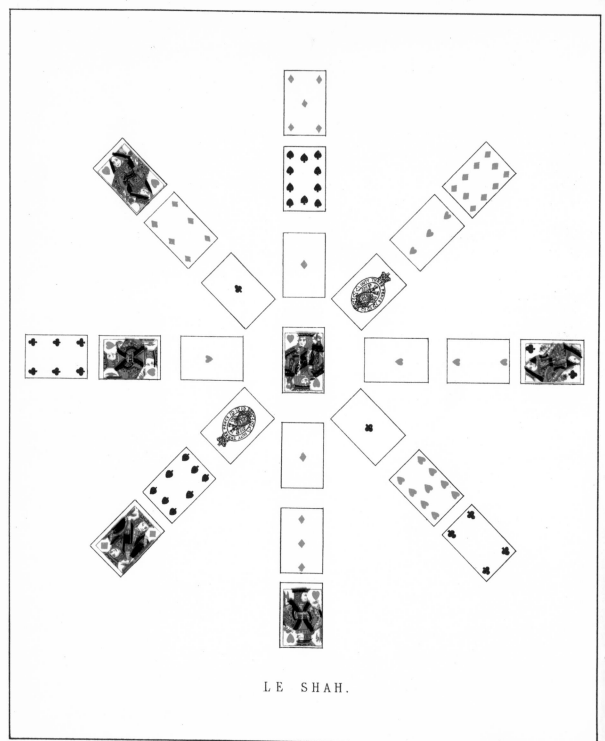

LE SHAH.

LE SHAH.

Two Entire Packs of Cards.

RULES.

I.   DURING the deal cards in each circle of the star are available until another circle blocks them.   After the deal is completed only cards in the third (or outer) circle are available until, as usual, their removal releases the inner circles.

II.   Marriages are limited to cards in the third circle ; cards in the inner circles, even when released, can only be played, but not married.

III.   The foundations must follow suit.

PLAY.

Take from the pack the eight aces and the eight kings.   Throw aside seven of the kings and place the remaining one in the centre, with the eight aces surrounding it in a circle.

The king is called The Shah, and remains alone.   The aces are the foundation cards, and are to ascend in sequence to queens.

Next deal out a circle of eight cards, beginning at the top and continuing from left to right.   If any of these are suitable, play them, filling the spaces at once from the cards in your hand.   Then deal out a second circle, blocking the first one (Rule I.), and treat it in the same manner, then a third circle, which completes the rays of the star.

Note.—In the pattern tableau the third circle is omitted for want of space.

You should now examine the star to see if there are any available cards· which it would be advantageous to marry, or to play (Rules I. and II.), but you are not obliged to do either until a favourable opportunity occurs. Marriages can only be made in descending line.

Note.—It is often better to wait until, in dealing, a card turns up likely to be soon required, and then by playing or marrying, you make a vacant space in which to place it.

When you have played or married all the cards you wish, the spaces so made must be re-filled from the talon or pack, beginning with the inner circles, and proceeding from left to right as before.

The remaining cards are dealt out in the usual way, those not required for the foundations, or for marrying, or for re-filling spaces, forming the talon.

When a lane, *i. e.* one entire ray of the star, is opened out, the place of the *inner* card may be filled by *one card* from the third circle. This is sometimes of great use, and is a kind of " grace," as this patience seldom succeeds. The other two spaces are re-filled from the talon, and this must be done at once, as each ray must always be complete.

There is no re-deal.

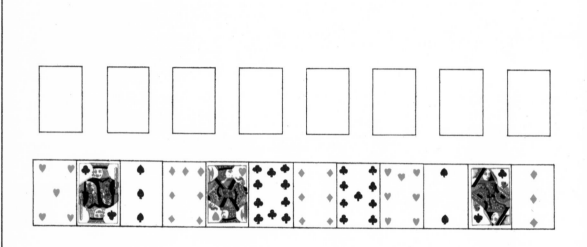

LE BLOCUS.

Vincent Brooks Day & Son lith

LE BLOCUS.

Two Entire Packs of Cards.

RULES.

I. ALL cards in the first row are available, but as each row is placed it blocks the preceding one.

The removal of any card in the lower rows releases the one immediately above it, the principle being that all cards are available that have *no others below them.*

II. The foundations must follow suit.

PLAY.

Deal out twelve cards in a horizontal line. Aces may be played as they appear, but no other card can be played until the row is complete. The eight aces are the foundation cards, and are to ascend in sequence to kings.

When the first line is placed, play any suitable cards, and then marry in descending line, but be careful to place the cards exactly over each other, to avoid confusion. The vacancies thus caused must be immediately re-filled from the pack, then again play and marry. When neither can be done, deal out another row underneath the first, and when it is complete, play, marry and refill spaces as before.

You continue to deal out successive rows until the pack is exhausted, always pausing between each row to play, marry and re-fill spaces.

In the course of the game vacancies will often be made in the higher rows. These must always be re-filled first.

There is no re-deal.

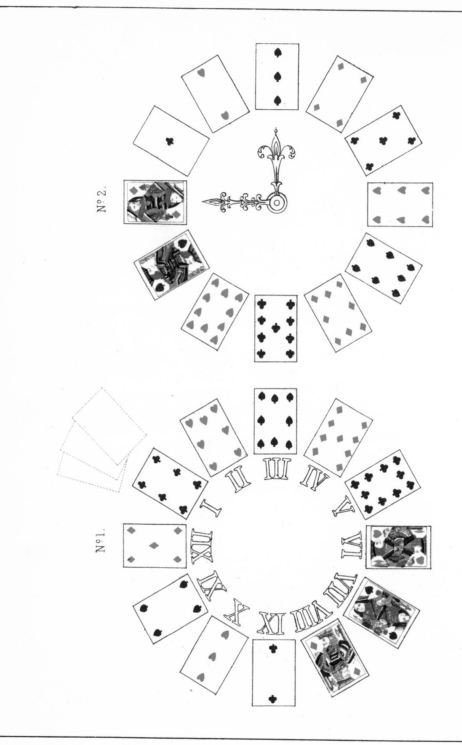

L'HORLOGE.

TABLEAU N°2 REPRESENTS THE PATIENCE WHEN FINISHED.

N°2.

N°1.

L'HORLOGE.

Two Entire Packs of Cards.

RULES.

I. WHEN the circle is formed, the uppermost cards of each packet are available, and their removal releases as usual those beneath.

II. Marriages can only be made with cards in the circle, and not with those from the pack or talon.

III. Vacancies in the circle must be re-filled with cards from the pack, but not from the talon; each packet must be re-filled so as to contain *not less* than three cards.

IV. The twelve foundations must follow suit.

PLAY.

Withdraw from the pack the twelve cards, as in tableau No. I., and place them in their exact order against the hours of the clock represented. These are the foundation cards, and are to ascend in sequence until each packet attains the hour of the clock against which it is placed.

Having placed these twelve foundations, proceed to deal out a circle consisting of twelve packets of three cards dealt together—so spread that each card is visible (see dotted line). From this circle you first play all suitable cards (Rule I.), and then marry in a descending line (Rule II.), and then re-fill spaces (Rule III.). This last should be done in order, from left to right, beginning at the numeral 1, and all the packets refilled before proceeding again to play, or to marry.

Note.—Although each packet must never contain less than the original number of three cards, they will often, by marriages, contain more.

You are not obliged to play cards which would be more useful if left on the circle.

When all further progress is at an end, deal out the remaining cards; play all suitable ones, then marry and re-fill spaces, but be careful not to infringe Rule II.

The cards that cannot be so employed are laid aside in one packet, forming the talon, which can only be used to play on the foundations.

There is no re-deal.

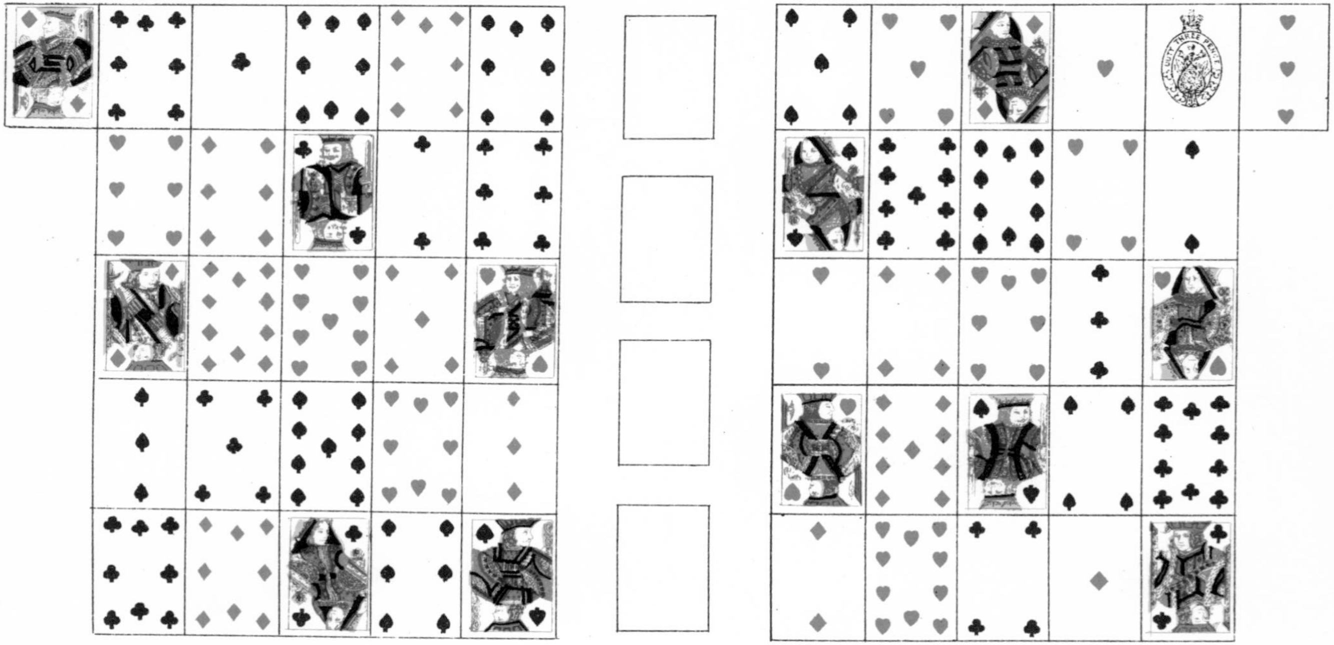

LA FORTERESSE..

LA FORTERESSE.

One Entire Pack of Cards.

RULES.

I. ONLY the outside cards of each group are available, until by their removal the next ones are released, the principle being that no card can be used *that has another outside it.*

Note.—By "outside" is meant the cards on the right side of the right hand group, and those on the left side of the left hand group.

II. The foundations must follow suit.

PLAY.

Deal out the entire pack horizontally in two groups, as in tableau, beginning at the left hand, and dealing straight across each group, leaving space in the centre for four aces. These, when they can be played, form the foundation cards, and are to ascend in sequence to kings.

Should any aces appear on the *outside* of either group, play them, as also any other suitable cards for continuing the foundations (Rules I. and II.).

You next proceed to form marriages, both in ascending and in descending lines, with cards on the outside of *both* groups (Rule I.). But this must be done with extreme care, so as not only to release the greatest number of suitable cards, but also, if possible, to open out one entire horizontal row of cards to form a lane. The success of the game entirely depends on these lanes. If, therefore, you succeed in opening out one, it is more prudent not to re-fill it, until by some fresh combination others can be made.

When a lane is to be re-filled, select any available card (Rule I.), and place it at the inner end of the lane, and along it any others in sequence of the same suit, the last card being of course the available one.

One great use of these lanes is, to reverse any sequences that have been made by marriages in the ascending line.

Note.—Supposing you have placed upon a deuce a sequence ending with eight; place the eight at the inner end of the lane, the other cards following in succession till the deuce becomes the outside card. When there are more cards in the lane than the original number they can be placed partly over each other.

There is no re-deal.

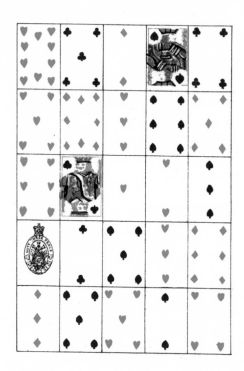

LES QUATORZE.

LES QUATORZE.

Two Entire Packs of Cards.

PLAY.

Deal out twenty-five cards in five rows, each containing five cards. The object is to compose the number fourteen with any two cards taken either from a perpendicular or from a horizontal row. The knave counts eleven, the queen twelve, and the king thirteen.

The cards so paired are withdrawn, and their places filled by the cards in your hand.

If in the course of the game the number fourteen cannot be composed, one chance remains—any two cards may be taken from their proper position, and may change places with any other two cards, and it is only in making this exchange, so as to produce one or more fourteens, that the player has any control over the success of the game, the success consisting of the entire pack being paired off. In the tableau three fourteens could be at once composed: The ten of hearts with the four of clubs, the knave of spades with the three of hearts, the eight of diamonds with the six of spades.

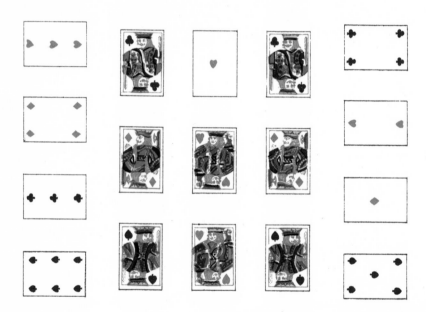

LE SULTAN

LE SULTAN.

Two Entire Packs of Cards.

RULE.

The foundations must follow suit.

PLAY.

Withdraw from the pack and place the eight kings and one ace of hearts as in tableau.

The centre king of hearts is called the Sultan, and remains alone. The other seven kings, with the ace of hearts, form the foundation cards. Each of these seven kings begins with ace, and ascends in sequence to queen. The ace of hearts ascends in the same manner, so that all the eight packets surrounding the Sultan end with queens.

You next deal out eight cards, four on either side (see tableau). These constitute the Divan. From this Divan you can play any suitable cards on the foundations, and having done so, proceed to deal out the remainder of the pack, turning the cards one by one, those that are not suitable for the foundations being laid aside in one packet forming the talon. Vacancies in the divan must be immediately re-filled from the talon, or when there is no talon, from the pack.

The talon may be taken up, shuffled and re-dealt if necessary twice.

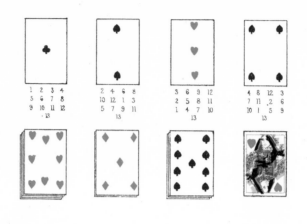

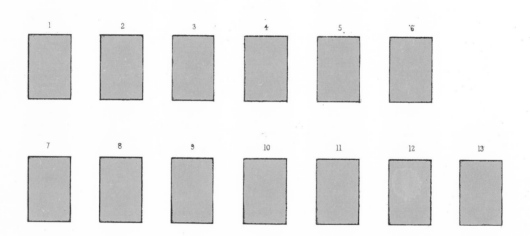

LE CALCUL.

Vincent Brooks Day & Son Lith

LE CALCUL.

One Entire Pack of Cards.

RULES.

I. THE foundations do not follow suit.

II. The talon may consist of four packets arranged at the player's discretion; but only the uppermost card of each is available, until those underneath are released in the usual manner.

PLAY.

Withdraw from the pack any ace, deuce, three, and four, and place them in a row, as in tableau. These are the foundation cards. The first or ace packet ascends in the usual sequence to king; the second packet ascends by twos, the third by threes, the fourth by fours—all the four packets terminating alike with kings.

In counting, the knave is reckoned as eleven, the queen as twelve, and the king as thirteen.

When, in forming the foundations, the number thirteen is passed (for it is never attained till it finishes each packet), the ace counts fourteen, the deuce fifteen, and so on. For example, in forming the second packet, when the number twelve or queen is reached, the next number required being fourteen, it is represented by ace, sixteen by three, and so on. This is difficult to describe, but may be understood by the numbers written on the tableau.

Having placed the foundations, deal out the cards in your hand, turning them one by one, playing all that are suitable on the foundations, the rest forming the talon (Rule II.).

On the judicious placing of this talon the success of the game depends, and a little practice is needed, to remember which cards will be required first, and to arrange the talon accordingly, for *a card once placed cannot be transferred from one packet to another.* The kings being wanted only to finish each foundation, it is advantageous to leave one packet for a time free to receive them; and, in forming the other packets, to avoid, as long as possible, covering the cards required first with those that will only be wanted later.

Note.—Some players wait, to place the foundation cards, until they appear in the course of the deal. This renders the game more interesting, but also more difficult, and in this manner it seldom succeeds.

There is no re-deal.

If this game should succeed, a sequel to it may be made as follows :— Take up the four foundation packets in order, placing the fourth on the third, the third on the second, and the second on the first, so that, on turning the cards to deal, the ace packet is uppermost.

Deal out thirteen cards in two horizontal rows, face downwards (see tableau, second part). Next deal a second round, *beginning on the second card* and continuing on *every alternate* card till all are covered; next deal a third round, *beginning on the third*, and continuing on *every third* card; next a fourth round *beginning on the fourth*, and continuing *on every fourth* card, each round, finishing on the thirteenth card.

Then turn the packets, and the cards will be found arranged, all of the same value together—four aces, four deuces, &c.

Note.—In the pattern tableau, No. 1, all the talon packets are represented as being established, but before that was done some of the foundations would probably have been already begun. The eight and the queen would at any rate have been played on the fourth foundation.

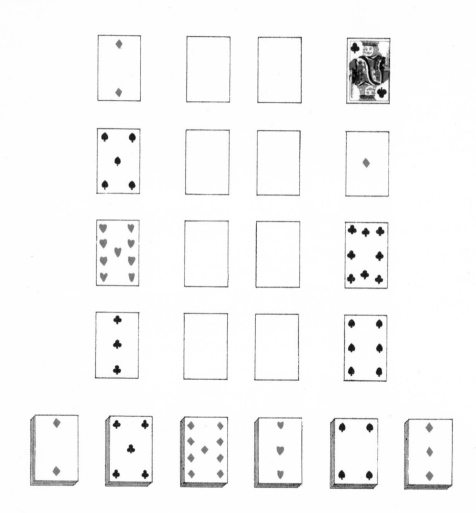

LA NIVERNAISE.

Vincent Brooks Day & Son Lith

LA NIVERNAISE.

Two Entire Packs of Cards.

RULES.

I. The Line is to consist of six packets, of which the uppermost card of each is alone available, until by its removal the one beneath is released—*the card which is uppermost at the time being always the available one.*

II. As many cards in each of the packets forming the Line may be examined as there are vacancies in the Flanks.

III. All the foundations must follow suit.

IV. In re-dealing, the Line packets must be taken up in succession, beginning on the left; then the whole together turned, and re-dealt as before.

PLAY.

Place two perpendicular rows of four cards each, called Flanks, leaving space in the centre for four aces and four kings of different suits. These, when they can be played, form the foundation cards, the kings descending in sequence to aces, the aces ascending in sequence to kings.

You next deal from left to right six packets, each composed of four cards dealt together, and placed in a horizontal line underneath. These packets are called the Line, and will receive successive additions.

If any of the foundation cards appear on the surface of the Line, or on the Flanks, play them in the spaces reserved; as also any other suitable cards subject to Rule I., taking, however, in preference, cards from the flanks, as the vacancies so made are most important.

Note.—So necessary to success are these vacancies that, if after dealing the first round of the Line none have been made, it is scarcely worth while to continue the game.

They may be filled from the pack or from the Line, but it is never prudent to fill up all vacancies; one at least should be left.

Single cards are not to be replaced on the Line; but if an entire packet has been played off, four more cards are to be immediately placed in its stead, and this rule applies to each several round.

When the resources thus far are exhausted, deal a second round of four cards together, on each of the Line packets as before, and continue thus to deal successive rounds until all the cards are dealt out, but between each round pause, and examine the Line (Rule II.) and the Flanks, and play all available cards.

The whole of the pack having been dealt, and further progress at an end, take up the Line as prescribed in Rule IV., re-deal, and play exactly as at first.

There is only one re-deal.

In forming the foundations, one card at a time may be exchanged from the ascending to the descending sequences, and *vice versâ*.

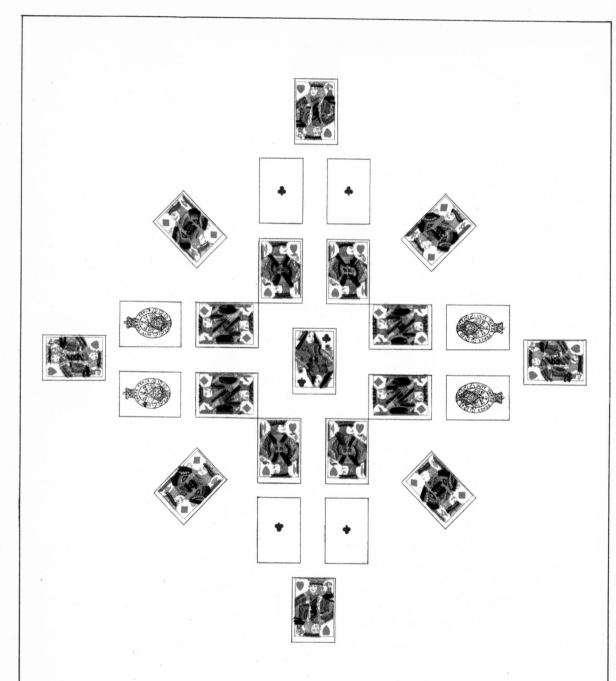

EMPRESS OF INDIA.

THE EMPRESS OF INDIA.

FOUR ENTIRE PACKS OF CARDS.

RULES.

I. ALL cards in the Army and Navy are equally available, if played in pairs (*i. e.* one black and one red), but no card of either colour can be played on a foundation *unless a card of the other colour is played at the same time on another foundation.*

II. Vacancies in the Army and Navy must be immediately re-filled with cards of their own colour from the talon, or when there is no talon, from the pack.

III. Cards from the pack or talon cannot be played at once, but must first pass through the Army or Navy.

IV. The talon consists of two packets, one of red, the other of black cards.

V. The foundations must follow suit.

PLAY.

Withdraw from the pack the eight black aces and the eight black queens, the eight red kings and the eight red knaves.

Place these cards as in the tableau, throwing aside the four queens of spades and three queens of clubs.

The remaining queen of clubs represents the Empress, the knaves the guard of British soldiers, and these nine cards remain alone.

The eight black aces and the eight red kings are the foundation cards, the aces ascending in sequence to kings, representing Admirals, the kings descending in sequence to aces, representing Generals.

Note.—The red sequences must omit knaves, the black ones must omit queens.

Deal out four horizontal rows, each containing twelve cards, of which the two upper rows are to be red (the Army), the two lower ones black (the Navy).

They are to be dealt at the same time, and if after the two rows of one colour, say red, are finished, more red cards turn up, they must be laid aside as a talon (Rule IV.).

When the Army and Navy are complete, if any available pairs of cards have been dealt (Rule I.) play them (the first pair must of course be a black two and a red queen), and re-fill the spaces ; but if there should be none, you may proceed to pair cards. Any card in the Army may be placed on any card in the Navy, and *vice versâ*, but the cards so paired cannot afterwards be separated, but must be played *at the same time* on their respective foundations. The vacancies thus made must be immediately re-filled (Rule II.).

Each card can only be paired once.

You may choose your own time for pairing cards. For instance, if you require say a ten of clubs for one of the foundations you may defer making a vacancy in the Navy until the ten of clubs is at the top of the talon. When you have played all available cards, deal out the remainder of the pack, those not required to fill vacancies being placed in two packets (Rule IV.).

There is no re-deal.

Note.—The Army and Navy could not be placed in the tableau from want of space.

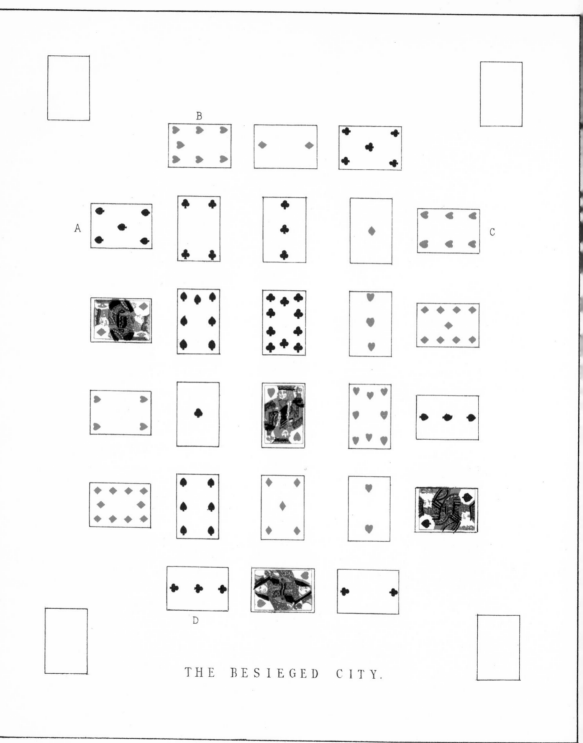

THE BESIEGED CITY.

THE BESIEGED CITY.

TWO ENTIRE PACKS OF CARDS.

RULES.

I. THE foundations are formed with cards from the Ramparts and from the pack. Cards from the talon must pass through the Reserve, and the Reserve must pass into the Ramparts before they can be played.

II. Cards in the Ramparts may be placed on each other either in the usual ascending and descending sequences, or in the order in which they will be played, viz. queen on two, knave on three, and so on, or *vice versâ*. They must be of the same suit; and sequences, both in ascending and in descending lines, may be placed in the same packet.

Cards in the Ramparts may be transferred from one packet to another at discretion (the top card of each being alone available), and they must follow suit.

III. Cards in the Reserve may in the same way be placed on those in the Ramparts, *but only on the cards at the ends or sides of the line* from which they are taken.

Note.—In the tableau the four of clubs could only be placed on cards at A, B, C, or D, and in this case only on D.

IV. Vacancies in the Ramparts are filled from the Reserve, with any card in the row at the end of which the vacancy occurs.

Note.—In the tableau a vacancy at B or D could only be filled by the four or ace of clubs, or by the seven or six of spades; and a vacancy at A or C, by the ace of diamonds or by the three or four of clubs.

V. Vacancies in the Reserve are filled from the talon, or when there is no talon, from the pack.

VI. The foundations must follow suit.

PLAY.

Deal twelve cards in four rows of three cards each. Then deal an *outside row* of fourteen cards placed crossways. These are the " Ramparts." The inside twelve cards are the " Reserve."

The foundation cards are four aces of different suits. On these are placed kings, then deuces, queens, threes and so on, each foundation consisting of alternate sequences, ascending and descending, and finishing as well as beginning with aces (Rule VI.).

Having placed the tableau, take from the Ramparts aces or other suitable cards (if any have been dealt) and play them in their allotted places, *immediately filling each vacancy as it occurs* (Rules IV. and V.); this must be done throughout the game. Then transfer cards in the Ramparts, and from the Reserve, as directed in Rules II. and III.

When you have done all that you wish (for it is optional), and again played if you can, deal out the remainder of the pack, the cards not suitable for the foundations being placed in a talon.

At the end of the patience, when the talon is exhausted and all the cards have been dealt, should there still be cards in the Reserve which cannot be transferred to the Ramparts, you may transpose them to effect this if you can.

This patience is exceedingly difficult.

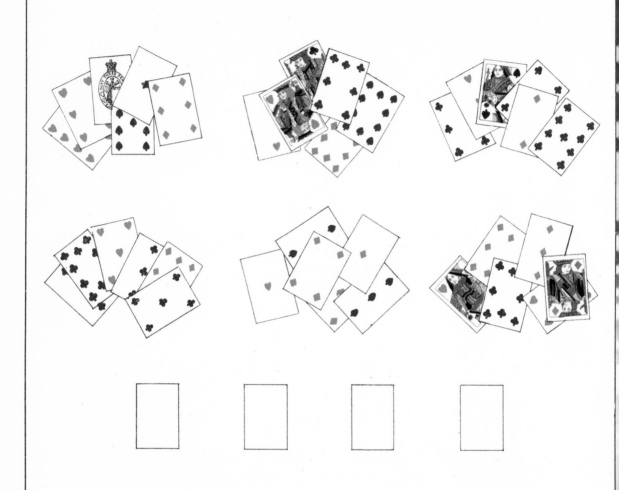

LE PARTERRE.

Vincent Brooks Day & Son. Lith.

LE PARTERRE.

ONE ENTIRE PACK OF CARDS.

RULES.

I. ANY card in the Bouquet and the uppermost cards of the Parterre are available. The removal of the top cards releases those beneath.

II. The foundations must follow suit.

III. Cards placed in sequence on the Parterre *need not* follow suit.

PLAY.

Deal six packets of six cards dealt together, and so spread that all are visible. The four aces are the foundation cards, and are to ascend in sequence to kings (Rule II.).

Sixteen cards will remain, which are called the Bouquet, and must be kept in the hand. Take from the Bouquet and from the Parterre any aces or other suitable cards (Rule I.) and play them.

Next place cards in descending sequences in the Parterre, transferring them from one packet to another as often as you please (Rules I. and III.), and you may place cards from the Bouquet in the same way.

For example, place the four of diamonds (see tableau) on the five of clubs, then take the ten of hearts from the Bouquet and place it on the knave of diamonds. The nine of clubs can now be transferred, and the ace and deuce of diamonds are released.

This patience is exceedingly difficult. Cards taken from the Bouquet cannot be returned to it, and there is only one deal. The greatest care must therefore be taken in placing cards in sequence and in playing them. You are not obliged to do either, and it is often better to leave a card than to play it, as it may be useful in releasing others.

When an entire packet is cleared off you may begin a new one with a card from the Bouquet or from the Parterre (Rule I.), and this is often the only means of removing a king, which, being the highest card, can never be transferred.

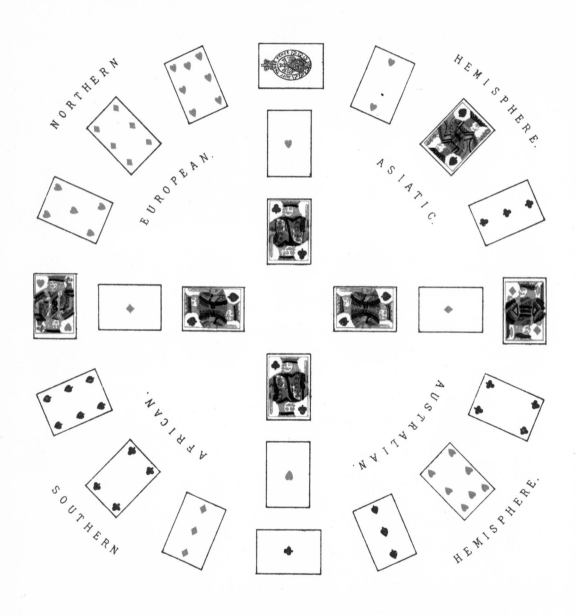

NORTHERN HEMISPHERE.

EUROPEAN. ASIATIC.

AFRICAN. AUSTRALIAN.

SOUTHERN HEMISPHERE.

LES HÉMISPHÈRES.

LES HÉMISPHÉRES.

Two Entire Packs of Cards.

RULES.

I. ONLY cards that belong to their proper hemisphere are available.

II. Cards of the wrong colours may be *exchanged* into their proper hemispheres whenever the opportunity occurs, and at the end of the game, when all the cards are dealt, and the talon is exhausted, they may be *transferred without an exchange*.

III. Cards may only marry those belonging to their own Race, but cards from the talon may marry those of any Race.

IV. The barriers cannot be moved till the end of the game, when they are played to complete the foundations.

V. All the foundations must follow suit.

PLAY.

Take from the pack and place as in tableau the four red aces and the four black kings.

Then place *crossways* a king of hearts and a king of diamonds, an ace of clubs and an ace of spades. The four latter cards are called barriers, and divide each Race.

The four black kings and the four red aces form the foundation cards, the aces ascending in sequence to kings, the kings descending in sequence to aces.

The red cards representing Europeans and Asiatics should inhabit the northern hemisphere, the black cards representing Australians and Africans the southern; but it is obvious that in dealing and re-filling vacancies, cards will often be found in the wrong hemispheres, *and while there they cannot be used in any way.*

Having placed the foundations and the barriers, deal out (from left to right, beginning from the king of hearts) a circle consisting of three cards between each barrier. These represent the four Races. From these Races you play, marry and exchange all available cards, subject to Rules I. II. III. and V.

Note.—The red suits marry in descending, the black in ascending line.

This done, you deal out the remainder of the pack, first re-filling vacancies in the Races (proceeding from left to right, as in the original deal) and then playing all suitable cards. The rest form the talon, from which cards may marry those in the circle, subject to Rules I. and III.

There is no re-deal.

LES PETITS PAQUETS.

LES PETITS PAQUETS.

Two Entire Packs of Cards.

RULES.

I. ANY card in the thirteenth packet, and the surface or uppermost cards of the twelve packets, are available. By the removal of the top cards those beneath are released in the usual manner.

II. Each foundation must follow suit.

III. In re-dealing, the twelve packets are to be taken up in order, six in one hand and six in the other (taking the right hand upper and the left hand lower rows alternately). Between the two groups place the thirteenth packet if any cards of it remain.

PLAY.

Withdraw from the pack and play the eight kings as in tableau. These are the foundation cards. The four kings in the upper row begin with aces, and ascend in sequence to queens; the kings in the lower row descend in sequence to aces.

Before proceeding, read the following directions to the end.

Deal out thirteen cards in two horizontal rows, the thirteenth card being placed a little apart. Then deal out a second round of thirteen cards to cover the first, and continue thus to deal out successive rounds until the pack is exhausted, the cards in the thirteenth packet being so spread that the whole are visible while the other twelve packets only show the surface card of each.

But in dealing each several round the following order of play is to be observed.

Each card is to be called by the numerical order in which it is dealt, irrespective of its actual value (the knave counting eleven, the queen twelve and the king thirteen). Whenever the actual value of any card corresponds to its number in the deal, that card is to be laid aside, face downwards, and is called the Exile (see tableau). When a card is thus laid aside, the next one in the pack must be placed in its stead, and the deal continued as before, invariably banishing as Exiles all those cards whose value and conventional number agree ; each round begins with number one and ends with thirteen.

The whole of the cards having been thus dealt out, examine all the thirteen packets (Rule I.), and play any available cards on the foundations.

When no more can thus be played, take the uppermost card of the Exiles and (if not suitable for any of the foundations) place it underneath the packet to whose conventional number its own value corresponds ; *i. e.* if the card is a five, slip it underneath the fifth packet, if a queen, under the twelfth, and so on. Then the top card of the same packet is to be treated in like manner (placed underneath the packet corresponding to its value), until by these changes of the surface cards a suitable one for any of the foundations is released.

Having played the card so released, and having again carefully examined the packets as before, playing all that are suitable, the next card of the Exiles must be taken, and the same process repeated until all the Exiles have been used.

The packets are then to be taken up in order (Rule III.), re-dealt (if necessary) twice, and played exactly as before.

In forming the foundations one card at a time may be exchanged from the ascending to the descending sequences, and *vice versâ.*

Note.—In the pattern tableau several rounds are represented to have been dealt, but in playing a game some of the foundations would by that time have been begun.

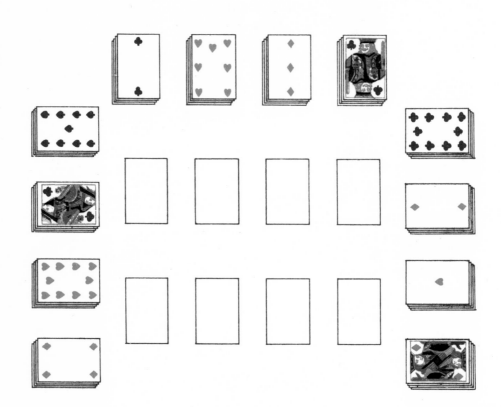

LE CARRÉ NAPOLÉON.

Vincent Brooks Day & Son Lith.

LE CARRÉ NAPOLÉON.

TWO ENTIRE PACKS OF CARDS.

RULES.

I. ONLY the uppermost cards of the packets in the square are available, until, by their removal, the cards underneath are released, but the whole of the square may be examined.

II. When a vacancy in the square is caused by the removal of an entire packet, the space may be filled by one card from the talon or pack, but this need not be done until a favourable opportunity occurs.

III. All the foundations must follow suit.

PLAY.

Deal out twelve packets, each consisting of four cards dealt together, so as to form three sides of a square, leaving space in the centre for the eight aces. These are the foundation cards, and are to ascend in sequence to kings.

If any aces appear on the surface of the square, play them in their allotted places, as also any other suitable cards.

You next proceed to form marriages in a descending line with the cards of the square, subject to Rule I. As usual, great judgment must be exercised in making these changes, lest cards underneath should be blocked by a sequence of higher cards of the same suit. If this were to occur in two packets, *i. e.* if in both cases sequences, say of diamonds, blocked lower cards of the same suit, success would be impossible.

Note.—If after dealing the square two kings of one suit were found to be blocking two smaller cards of that suit, either the whole must be taken up and re-dealt, or one king must be slipped underneath.

You now proceed to play out the rest of the cards, those that are not suitable for the foundations or for the sequences of the square being placed in a talon.

There is no re-deal.

This game may be also played as follows :—

Deal out a square of twelve *single* cards, then deal the rest of the pack as usual, the cards that are suitable being played on the foundations or married (in descending line) to those on the square, ready to be transferred to the foundations, the rest placed in a talon, and vacancies filled in the usual manner.

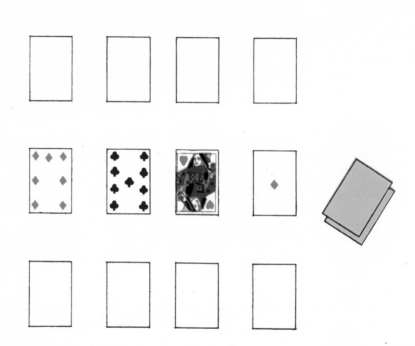

LA DUCHESSE DE LUYNES.

LA DUCHESSE DE LUYNES.

Two Entire Packs of Cards.

RULES.

I. The uppermost cards of each of the packets are available, as are also those below, when the cards covering them are removed. The Discard is only available at the end of each deal.

II. The foundations must follow suit.

PLAY.

Deal out in a horizontal row four cards face upwards, then place two cards apart face downwards. These latter are the Discard. Four aces and four kings of different suits form the foundations, the aces ascending in sequence to kings, the kings descending in sequence to aces.

When any of these foundation cards appear in the course of the deal, play them in their allotted spaces (the aces above, the kings below), as also any other suitable cards, subject to Rule I.

Having dealt this first round, proceed to deal successive rounds, each covering the preceding one, and adding two cards each time to the Discard. Between every round pause, and play all suitable cards on the foundations. The spaces so made are never to be re-filled until the succeeding round of cards is placed which naturally covers them.

When the entire pack is exhausted take up the Discard, examine it, and play from it all suitable cards on the foundations, of course adding, as before, any from the surface of the four packets.

When further progress is at an end, take up the four packets in succession, placing the Discard underneath, and re-deal the whole as before, playing it exactly in the same manner.

There may be three re-deals, but in the last or fourth deal no Discard is placed.

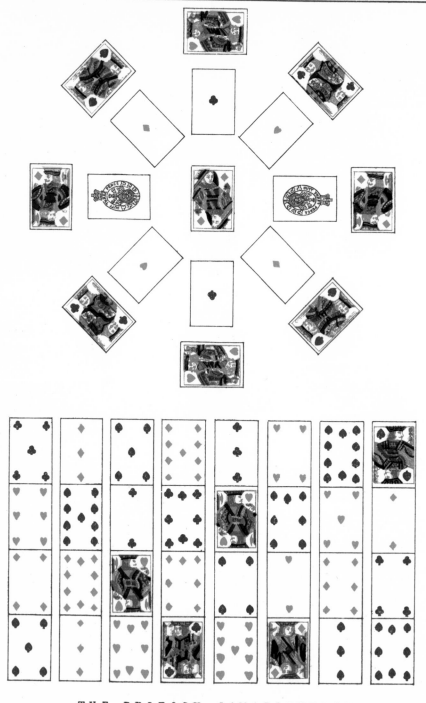

THE BRITISH CONSTITUTION.

THE BRITISH CONSTITUTION.

Two Entire Packs of Cards.

RULES.

I. The foundations are formed exclusively from the "Privy Council." All cards in the other divisions, pack, or talon, must ascend through each division till they reach the top before they can be played.

II. Cards in the three lower divisions may be placed in sequence on cards in the next division above them, and in this manner they may be transferred from one division to another till they reach the top.

III. When cards are placed in sequence in the "Constitution," the top card only of each sequence is available until its removal releases the one beneath.

IV. All sequences must be of alternate colours, and in descending line—*i. e.* a red nine on a black ten, then a black eight, a red seven, and so on. Any number of cards may be so placed.

V. Each vacancy must be *at once* filled by a card from the division immediately below it; and as this rule applies equally to all the rows, a vacancy will thus be caused in the lowest row or "People," which must be filled from the talon, or, when there is no talon, from the pack.

VI. The foundations must follow suit.

PLAY.

Take from the pack the kings, queens, and aces—seven of the queens are to be thrown aside, and the other cards placed as in tableau.

The queen of diamonds represents THE SOVEREIGN, the black kings the Bishops, the red kings the Judges.

The eight aces form the foundation cards or "Government," and ascend in sequence to knaves.

Deal out four horizontal rows (beginning with the lowest), each containing eight cards.

This forms the "Constitution." Each row represents a separate division.

The first (or lowest row) is the "People," the second the "House of Commons," the third the "House of Lords," the last the "Privy Council."

When the tableau is complete, if any suitable cards are to be found in the "Privy Council" row, play them (Rule I.), immediately re-filling each vacancy as it is made (Rule V.).

You must then examine the Constitution to see which cards may be most advantageously placed in sequence (Rules II. and IV.).

Note.—The success of this game depends chiefly on the play. In filling a vacancy choose the card (Rule V.) which has the most chance of reaching the top, or of being useful to cards in the row below it. It is often better to defer making a vacancy till a card turns up in dealing that is required.

When you have played all available cards and placed in sequence all that you wish, deal out the remainder of the pack, the cards not required to fill vacancies in the "People" forming the talon.

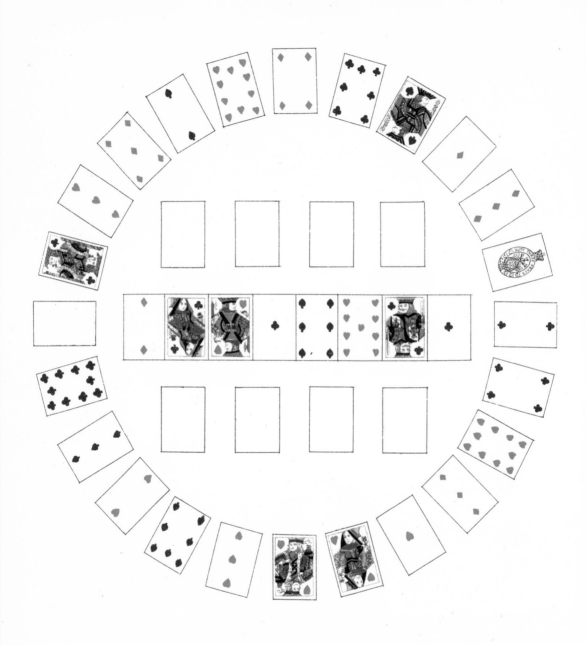

LE ZODIAC.

Vincent Brooks Day & Son Lith

THE ZODIAC.

Two Entire Packs of Cards.

RULES.

I. MARRIAGES may be made in the Zodiac with cards from the Equator (but not *vice versâ*) and from the talon or pack, but cards in the Zodiac cannot marry each other, neither can those in the Equator do so. Marriages may be made in ascending and descending lines, and the same packet may contain both.

II. The foundations must follow suit.

PLAY.

Deal eight cards in a horizontal row called the "Equator." Then deal a surrounding circle of twenty-four cards called the "Zodiac."

The foundations are not formed *till the end of the game.* They are to consist of the four aces and four kings of different suits, the aces ascending in sequence to kings, the kings descending in sequence to aces.

Having placed the tableau, you proceed to marry (Rule I.) and to re-fill the spaces from the talon, or, where there is no talon, from the pack, but you are not obliged to do either until a favourable opportunity occurs. You continue to deal out the cards in the usual way, those not required for marrying or for re-filling spaces forming the talon. This is to be re-dealt as often as required—that is, until all the cards are placed either in the Zodiac or in the Equator. If this cannot be done the patience has already failed. If you succeed in placing all the cards you then begin to form the eight foundations from the Zodiac and Equator (Rule II.).

It is obvious that the greatest care is required in marrying the cards, or you will so block them as to be unable to form the foundations.

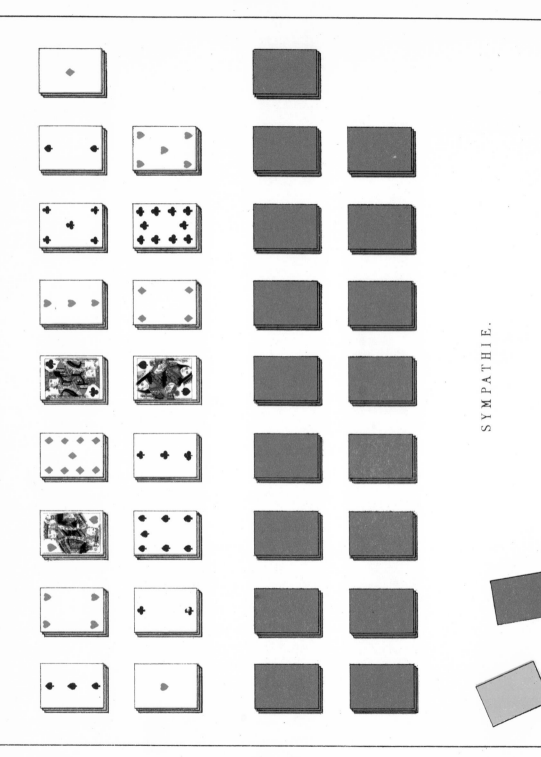

S Y M P A T H I E .

SYMPATHIE.

FOR TWO PLAYERS.

TWO ENTIRE PACKS OF CARDS.

PLAY.

EACH player takes one of the packs, and deals it in packets of three cards together, face downwards; each player will thus have seventeen packets, and one card over as a " grace."

The first player now turns the uppermost card of each of his packets, or if preferred, he may in dealing turn these cards. See tableau.

When this has been done, the second player proceeds to turn the uppermost cards of each of his packets, one by one, and whenever a card so turned corresponds in value and suit with any upturned card of the first player, both the cards thus paired are withdrawn and laid aside by their respective owners, and the next card of the packet from which the successful one was taken, is paired if possible in the same manner. This process is repeated till the uppermost card of each of the packets is face upwards.

The first player having now some packets face downwards, proceeds to turn the uppermost cards in the same manner, and to pair

them when possible.   Each player continues this process alternately
until further progress is at an end.   Then each has recourse by
turns to his "grace," after which, if any cards remain on the table
unturned, the game has failed, and "Sympathie" between the players
has not been established.